The Nature Kid's Guide to
BUTTERFLIES

DAVID ANDERSON

LP Media Inc. Publishing
Text copyright © 2026 by LP Media Inc.

For information address LP Media Inc. Publishing,
30012 Variolite St NW, Princeton MN 55371
www.lpmedia.org

Publication Data

Butterflies
The Nature Kid's Guide to Butterflies — First edition.

Summary: "Learn all about Butterflies, the Nature Kid Way"
— Provided by publisher.

ISBN: 979-8-89818-191-8

[1. Butterflies – Non-Fiction] I. Title.

Title: The Nature Kid's Guide to Butterflies

CONTENTS

BUTTERFLY BONANZA

The western pygmy blue butterfly is smaller than a penny. It could sit on your fingernail!

Flutter! A Monarch butterfly lands on a purple flower.

Look up! That flash of color dancing through the air is one of the most beautiful creatures on Earth. It is a butterfly!

Butterflies live almost everywhere in the world, on every continent except frozen Antarctica. There are about 20,000 different kinds. Some are as big as your hand. Others are smaller than your thumbnail.

Those stunning wings are covered in thousands of tiny scales, like a painting made by nature. Some butterflies glow orange and black. Others flash brilliant blue, green, or white. No two species look exactly alike, and every single one is worth stopping to admire.

BRILLIANT BODIES

Whoosh! Tiny scales shimmer as a butterfly zooms past.

A butterfly has three body parts. It has a head, a chest, and a belly. Two thin feelers called antennae sit on its head.

Four wide wings help it fly. Tiny scales cover each wing like shingles on a roof. These scales create bright colors and patterns. Touch them and they rub off like dust.

Butterflies have six thin legs, and they can actually taste with their feet! When a butterfly lands on a flower, it knows right away if the **nectar** is sweet.

A butterfly has about 12,000 tiny lenses packed into two big compound eyes!

MAGICAL CATERPILLARS

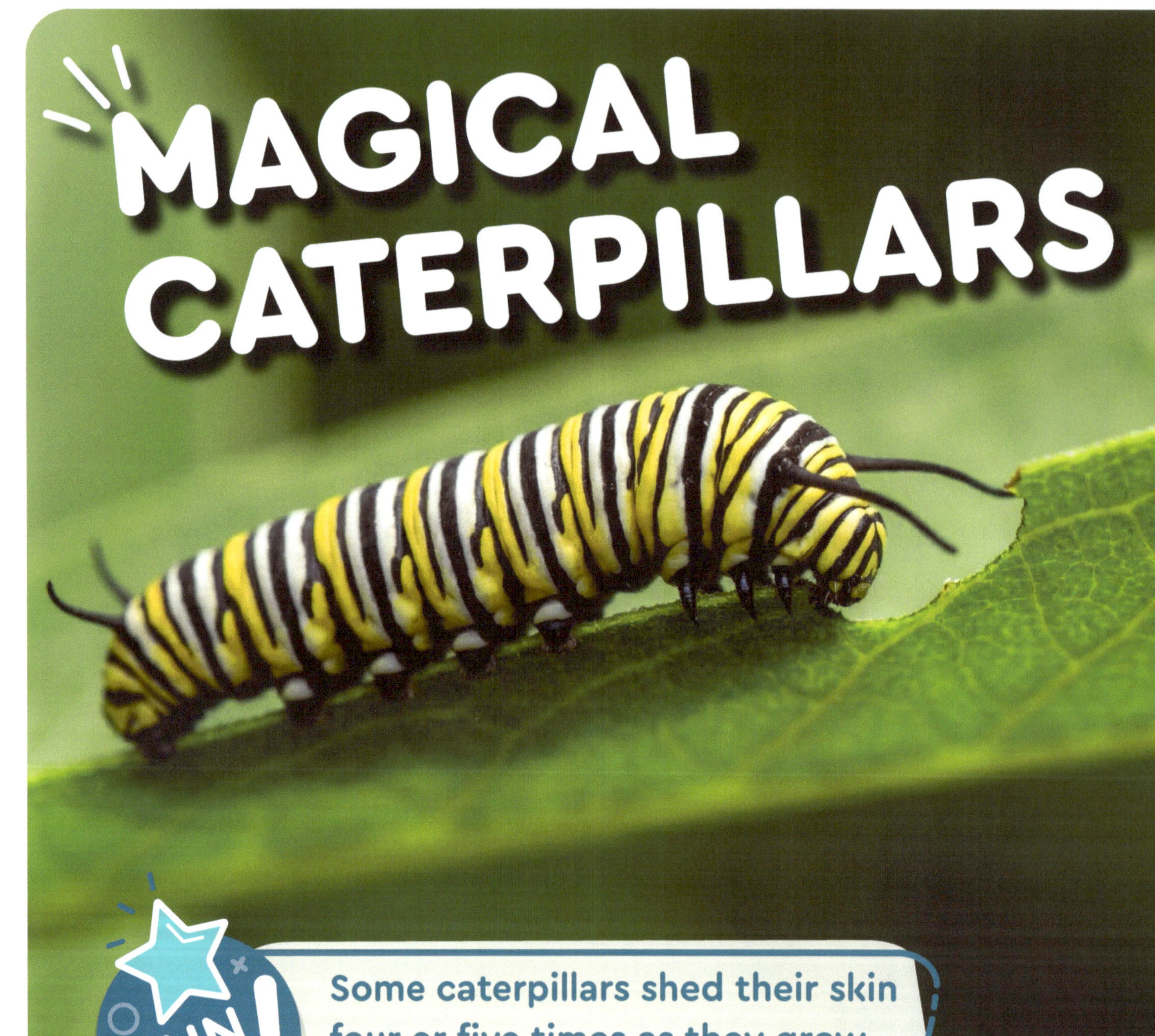

Some caterpillars shed their skin four or five times as they grow bigger!

Munch! A tiny caterpillar nibbles on a milkweed leaf.

Every butterfly starts as a tiny egg. A mother butterfly lays her eggs on a leaf. Soon a caterpillar hatches and starts to eat.

The caterpillar eats and grows fast. It munches leaves all day long. When it is big enough, it forms a hard shell called a **chrysalis**. Inside, something amazing happens.

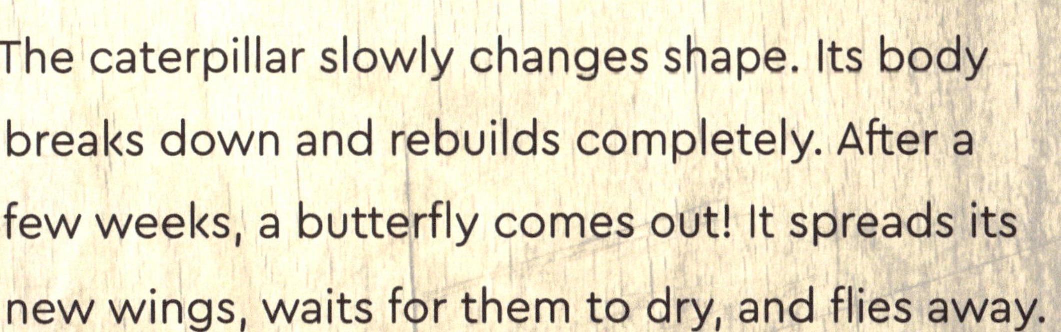

The caterpillar slowly changes shape. Its body breaks down and rebuilds completely. After a few weeks, a butterfly comes out! It spreads its new wings, waits for them to dry, and flies away.

SIPPING SECRETS

Slurp! A butterfly unrolls its long tube for a sweet drink.

Butterflies do not chew food. Instead, they sip it through a long, thin tube called a **proboscis**. This tube curls up tight like a party horn when not in use.

When a butterfly lands on a flower, it unrolls its tube. Then it sips nectar from deep inside the bloom. Nectar is a sweet juice that flowers make just for visitors like butterflies.

Some butterflies also visit mud puddles to drink. This behavior is called puddling, and it is more important than it sounds. Mud contains salts and minerals that butterflies cannot get from nectar alone. These nutrients help them grow strong, fly farther, and even lay healthier eggs.

SURVIVAL SECRETS

Flash! A butterfly snaps open its wings to scare a bird away.

Butterflies have many ways to stay safe. Some flash bright colors to warn birds. These colors say, "I taste bad—don't eat me!"

Others hide by blending in. Their wings may look like dead leaves or rough bark. When they close their wings, they seem to vanish.

A few butterflies fly in zigzag paths to escape hungry beaks. Others drop to the ground and play dead. Staying alive takes lots of clever tricks!

WORLD TRAVELERS

Swoop! Thousands of butterflies take off on a very long trip.

Many butterflies stay in one place all year. But some take long trips called **migration**. They fly far to find warm weather and food.

Monarch butterflies fly all the way from Canada to Mexico every fall. That is up to 3,000 miles! Painted lady butterflies travel even farther. Scientists think they may fly up to 9,000 miles, making their trip the longest of any butterfly in the world.

How do they find their way? Butterflies use the sun as a compass. Some can even sense Earth's magnetic pull. These tiny travelers are amazing navigators.

MOTH MYSTERIES

Fwip! A fuzzy moth bumps into the porch light at night.

Moths and butterflies are close cousins. They both have wings covered in tiny scales. But look closely—they are not the same!

Most moths come out at night. Most butterflies fly during the day. Moths have thick, fuzzy bodies. Butterflies are thin and smooth.

Check their feelers too. Butterfly feelers have a little knob at the tip. Moth feelers look feathery or plain. Now you can tell them apart!

There are about 160,000 kinds of moths but only 20,000 kinds of butterflies!

MONARCH MIGRATION

Monarch butterflies are easy to spot. They have bright orange wings with bold black lines. White dots line the edges like tiny pearls.

Monarchs need a plant called milkweed. Mothers lay eggs only on its leaves. The caterpillars eat the milkweed, and it makes them taste terrible to birds.

Each fall, millions of monarchs crowd into trees in Mexico to stay warm. They hang from branches in huge orange clusters. When spring arrives, new monarchs fly back north to start the cycle again.

MORPHO MAGIC

Flick! A bright blue wing catches the light in the rain forest.

Blue morpho butterflies live in rain forests. You can find them in Central and South America. Their wings flash a brilliant, electric blue.

But here is a secret—the wings are not really blue! Tiny ridges on the scales bounce light in a special way. This trick creates the dazzling color we see.

When a morpho closes its wings, the bottom side shows brown with eyespots. This helps it blend in with dead leaves on the forest floor. A hungry bird may fly right past without noticing.

SWALLOWTAIL SPLENDOR

Zoom! A swallowtail sails past with its long tail-like wings.

Swallowtail butterflies are named for their tails. Their back wings have long, pointed tips that look like the tail of a swallow bird.

There are over 550 kinds of swallowtails around the world. Many have yellow and black stripes. Others glow blue, green, or white with bright spots.

You can see swallowtails in gardens, meadows, and forests. They are some of the biggest butterflies around. Watch for them gliding on warm summer days.

PAINTED WANDERERS

Swish! A painted lady flutters from one pink flower to the next.

Painted lady butterflies live almost everywhere. You can find them on every **continent** except Antarctica and Australia. No other butterfly lives in so many places!

Their wings are orange and brown with black spots. White dots line the wing tips. They look a bit like monarchs, but with a different pattern.

Painted ladies are always on the move. They can show up in almost any garden or field. You might spot one in your own yard today!

One painted lady was tracked flying over 9,000 miles across the Atlantic Ocean!

INVISIBLE WINGS

Zip! A glasswing butterfly darts past on its clear wings.

Glasswing butterflies have see-through wings. You can look right through them like a window! They live in the rain forests of Central and South America.

Their clear wings help them hide from birds. It is hard to catch something you can barely see. They seem to vanish into thin air.

Glasswings have dark edges and small splashes of color on their wings. That is all you see as they flutter past. The rest of the wing is invisible.

BIRDWING GIANTS

Queen Alexandra's birdwing is so rare that selling one is against the law!

Thwap! Giant wings beat the air like a small bird flying past.

Birdwing butterflies are the biggest in the world. Some have wings that stretch up to 12 inches wide. That is as wide as a dinner plate! When one glides through the forest, it looks more like a small bird than a butterfly.

These stunning insects live in the rainforests of Asia and Australia. Their wings glow with bold patterns of green, yellow, and black. Males are smaller, but have the brightest colors.

Birdwings need tall trees and thick forests to survive. When forests are cut down, they lose their homes. Many kinds are now rare and protected by law.

OWL EYES

FUN FACT!
An owl butterfly's eyespots can be
as big as a real pygmy owl's eyes!

Blink! Two huge eyespots stare up from a butterfly's wings.

Owl butterflies have big spots on their wings. These spots look just like owl eyes. They can scare away birds and lizards that want to eat them.

These butterflies are quite large. Their wings can stretch six inches wide. They live in rain forests in Central and South America.

Owl butterflies come out at dawn and dusk. They stay hidden during bright daylight. Their dark brown wings help them blend into the shadows of the forest.

STRIPED SURVIVOR

Flit! Black and yellow stripes drift through the warm air.

Zebra longwing butterflies have long, narrow wings. They are striped black and yellow, just like a zebra. You can spot them in warm, wet places.

These butterflies live in the southern United States and Central America. They like shady forests and gardens. Watch them glide along in a slow, graceful way.

What makes them special? They eat pollen as well as nectar. This extra protein helps them live up to six months, which is much longer than most butterflies!

LEAFY DISGUISE

34

Crunch! A butterfly lands on a branch and looks just like a leaf.

The dead leaf butterfly has one of the best disguises in nature. With its wings closed, it looks exactly like a dry brown leaf — complete with veins, spots, and even a fake stem mark on the edges. A hungry bird could land right next to one and never notice it at all.

But open those wings and see a surprise! The top side flashes bright orange and blue. It is a hidden burst of color that only appears in flight.

These butterflies live in forests across Asia. Their leaf trick keeps them safe from hungry birds. After all, no bird would peck at a dry old leaf!

NATURE'S HELPERS

Flutter! A butterfly dusts a flower with pollen and moves on to the next.

Butterflies are more than just pretty wings. As they sip nectar from flower to flower, they carry pollen on their bodies. This helps plants make seeds. Without butterflies, many of the flowers, fruits, and plants that people and animals depend on could not survive.

Butterflies are also a sign of a healthy place. When they are thriving, it means the plants, soil, and air around them are healthy too. When they disappear, it is nature's way of telling us something is wrong.

BUTTERFLY RESCUE

Rustle! A cloud of colorful butterflies rises into the blue sky.

Many butterflies are in trouble today. Forests are cut down, pesticides hurt them, and meadows are replaced by parking lots. Changes in weather make life even harder for these fragile insects.

But people are fighting back. Gardens full of nectar-rich flowers are being planted in backyards and schoolyards everywhere.

You can help too. Help your parents plant zinnias, coneflowers, and milkweed. Then on a warm sunny day, sit very still outside. You just might feel the tiny flutter of wings as a butterfly lands right beside you.

GLOSSARY

proboscis
A long, hollow tube a butterfly uses to sip nectar from flowers

chrysalis
A hard case where a caterpillar changes into a butterfly

continent
One of the seven large land areas on Earth

migration
A long trip animals take to find food or warmth

nectar
Sweet juice inside flowers that butterflies drink